OMB Sequestration Preview Report to the President and Congress for Fiscal Year 2016

February 2, 2015

TABLE OF CONTENTS

PAGE

Transmittal Letter

I.	Introduction	1
II.	Discretionary Sequestration Preview Report	3

GENERAL NOTES

1. All years referred to are fiscal years unless otherwise noted.

2. Details in the tables and text may not add to totals due to rounding.

EXECUTIVE OFFICE OF THE PRESIDENT
OFFICE OF MANAGEMENT AND BUDGET
WASHINGTON, D.C. 20503

THE DIRECTOR

February 2, 2015

The President
The White House
Washington, D.C. 20500

Dear Mr. President:

Enclosed please find the *OMB Sequestration Preview Report to the President and Congress for Fiscal Year 2016*. It has been prepared pursuant to section 254 of the Balanced Budget and Emergency Deficit Control Act of 1985 (BBEDCA), as amended.

As required by law, the Preview Report, the first of the three required sequestration reports for 2016, sets forth estimates for the current year and each subsequent year through 2021 of the applicable discretionary spending limits for each category. These estimates include any adjustments based on current law, including the adjustments that are calculated in the *OMB Report to the Congress on the Joint Committee Reductions for Fiscal Year 2016*, and adjustments due to changes in concepts and definitions. The report also provides a summary of the proposed and anticipated changes to the discretionary spending limits included in the 2016 Budget.

Sincerely,

Shaun Donovan
Director

Enclosure

Identical Letter Sent to The Honorable Joseph R. Biden, Jr.
and The Honorable John A. Boehner

I. INTRODUCTION

The Budget Control Act of 2011 (BCA) amended the Balanced Budget and Emergency Deficit Control Act of 1985 (BBEDCA), which had expired in 2002, by reinstating limits on discretionary budget authority for 2012 through 2021. The 2013 and 2014 limits were revised by the American Taxpayer Relief Act of 2012 (ATRA), and the 2014 and 2015 limits were further revised by the Bipartisan Budget Act of 2013 (BBA).

Section 254 of BBEDCA requires OMB to issue a sequestration preview report with the President's Budget submission. This preview report, the first of the three required sequestration reports for 2016, provides the status of the discretionary limits for the current year and each year thereafter through 2021 as of the end of the second session of the 113th Congress based on current law. At this time, section 251A of BBEDCA requires an adjustment to the budget year (2016) caps in this report based on the calculations included in the *OMB Report to the Congress on the Joint Committee Reductions for Fiscal Year 2016*. Unlike last year, when the BBA was enacted, no legislation has been enacted that replaces the Joint Committee reductions to the caps for discretionary programs in 2016 and beyond. This report also describes the President's proposals to increase the 2016 discretionary caps and replace most of the discretionary cap reductions scheduled to take place in 2017 through 2021 while extending the discretionary caps through 2025.

OMB will issue a sequestration update report in August that will provide a mid-year status update on the limits and enacted appropriations, as well as a preview estimate of the 2016 adjustment for disaster funding. OMB will issue a final sequestration report for 2016 after the end of this congressional session that will contain final estimates of enacted appropriations and any adjustments to the discretionary limits. If it is determined that a cap has been breached, the final report will also include a Presidential Order to implement a sequestration of non-exempt discretionary accounts within that category to eliminate the breach. As required by BBEDCA, OMB's estimates of enacted discretionary appropriations and the calculations in each sequestration report, including this preview report, are made using the same economic and technical assumptions underlying the most recent President's Budget. In addition, each of these reports will include, where appropriate, comparisons between OMB's estimates and estimates from the Congressional Budget Office and an explanation of any differences between those estimates.

II. DISCRETIONARY SEQUESTRATION PREVIEW REPORT

Discretionary programs are funded annually through the appropriations process. BBEDCA limits—or caps—budget authority available for discretionary programs each year through 2021 but does not require that the Congress appropriate the full amount available under the discretionary limits. Throughout each session of the Congress, OMB is required to monitor compliance with the discretionary spending limits. Within seven working days of enactment of an appropriations bill, OMB reports its estimates of the total discretionary budget authority and outlays provided by the legislation. If the bill provides additional appropriations for the current year, OMB also determines at that time whether the additional budget authority would cause total discretionary appropriations to exceed the relevant cap for that year. OMB makes the same determination for the budget year at the end of each session of the Congress. Appropriations that OMB estimates exceed the budget authority caps trigger an across-the-board reduction (or sequestration) to eliminate the excess spending. However, if the caps for the current year are breached late in the fiscal year (after June 30), the caps for the following budget year are reduced by the amount of the excess.

Section 251 of BBEDCA originally specified for 2012 and 2013 separate "security" and "nonsecurity" categories[1] for discretionary programs and then a single category for all discretionary spending referred to as the "discretionary" category for each year after 2013. Section 302 of the BCA revised these caps because the Congress failed to enact legislation to reduce the deficit by more than $1.2 trillion by January 15, 2012. The revised security category was defined to include only the discretionary programs in the defense budget function (050) (the "defense" category), which mainly consists of the Department of Defense and significant portions of agency budgets for the Department of Energy (including the National Nuclear Security Administration) and the Federal Bureau of Investigation. The revised non-security category was defined to consist of all discretionary programs not in the revised security category—essentially all non-defense (non-050) budget functions (the "non-defense" category). Although ATRA reinstated the security and nonsecurity categories for 2013 at lower levels, the defense and non-defense categories were left in place for 2014 through 2021 and were continued in the BBA.

Section 251A of BBEDCA requires an annual reduction in the caps as part of the Joint Committee reductions. In OMB's Sequestration Preview Report for 2014[2], the 2014 defense cap was reduced by $53.9 billion and the non-defense cap was reduced by $36.6 billion. The BBA restored $22.4 billion each ($44.8 billion in total) to the defense and non-defense categories for 2014. The BBA also cancelled the Joint Committee reductions to the defense and non-defense caps that would have taken place for 2015 and instead reduced the defense cap by $44.7 billion and the non-defense cap by $27.6 billion from the original BCA levels. The BBA, however, did not cancel Joint Committee reductions after 2015 and, since there has been no further congressional action, section 251A of BBEDCA now requires a reduction to the discretionary caps for 2016 similar to those that occurred in 2014 and were reflected in OMB's Sequestration Preview Report for 2014. The 2016 annual reductions are made in this report (see the current law adjustments section below). Any reductions in 2017 through 2021 will be made when OMB issues its Joint Committee and sequestration preview reports for each of those years. Furthermore, the precise amount of those reductions is unknown at this time as it depends in part on the relative size of sequestrable mandatory outlays in the baseline for those Budgets. Therefore, those future cap reductions are not reflected in the revised limits used in this report.

Table 1 summarizes the history of changes that have occurred to the discretionary caps since their reinstatement and subsequent redefinition in the

---

[1] For more information on the structure of the original security and nonsecurity categories, see any of OMB's sequestration reports to the President and Congress for fiscal years 2012 through 2014 on OMB's website: *http://www.whitehouse.gov/omb/legislative_reports/sequestration*.

[2] See "OMB Sequestration Preview Report to the President and Congress for Fiscal Year 2014 and OMB Report to the Congress on the Joint Committee Reductions for Fiscal Year 2014 (Corrected Version)" on OMB's website for more information: *http://www.whitehouse.gov/omb/legislative_reports/sequestration*.

Table 1. OVERVIEW OF CHANGES TO DISCRETIONARY SPENDING LIMITS AND THE PRESIDENT'S PROPOSED LIMITS IN THE 2016 BUDGET

(Discretionary budget authority in billions of dollars)

	2012	2013	2014	2015	2016	2017	2018	2019	2020	2021	2022	2023	2024	2025
Original limits set in Title I of the Budget Control Act of 2011:														
Security Category	684.0	686.0	N/A	N/A	N/A	N/A	N/A	N/A	N/A	N/A	N/A	N/A	N/A	N/A
Nonsecurity Category	359.0	361.0	N/A	N/A	N/A	N/A	N/A	N/A	N/A	N/A	N/A	N/A	N/A	N/A
Discretionary Category	N/A	N/A	1,066.0	1,086.0	1,107.0	1,131.0	1,156.0	1,182.0	1,208.0	1,234.0	N/A	N/A	N/A	N/A
Redefinition of limits pursuant to section 251A of BBEDCA:														
Security Category	......	−686.0	N/A	N/A	N/A	N/A	N/A	N/A	N/A	N/A	N/A	N/A	N/A	N/A
Nonsecurity Category	......	−361.0	N/A	N/A	N/A	N/A	N/A	N/A	N/A	N/A	N/A	N/A	N/A	N/A
Discretionary Category	N/A	N/A	−1,066.0	−1,086.0	−1,107.0	−1,131.0	−1,156.0	−1,182.0	−1,208.0	−1,234.0	N/A	N/A	N/A	N/A
Defense Category	N/A	+546.0	+555.0	+566.0	+577.0	+590.0	+603.0	+616.0	+630.0	+644.0	N/A	N/A	N/A	N/A
Non-Defense Category	N/A	+501.0	+510.0	+520.0	+530.0	+541.0	+553.0	+566.0	+578.0	+590.0	N/A	N/A	N/A	N/A
Adjustments to limits pursuant to section 901(d) of ATRA:														
Security Category	......	+684.0	N/A	N/A	N/A	N/A	N/A	N/A	N/A	N/A	N/A	N/A	N/A	N/A
Nonsecurity Category	......	+359.0	N/A	N/A	N/A	N/A	N/A	N/A	N/A	N/A	N/A	N/A	N/A	N/A
Defense Category	N/A	−546.0	−4.0	N/A	N/A	N/A	N/A	N/A	N/A	N/A	N/A	N/A	N/A	N/A
Non-Defense Category	N/A	−501.0	−4.0	N/A	N/A	N/A	N/A	N/A	N/A	N/A	N/A	N/A	N/A	N/A
Joint Select Committee on Deficit Reduction Enforcement:														
Defense Category	N/A	N/A	−53.9	−44.7	−53.9	......	......	......	......	......	......	......	......	......
Non-Defense Category	N/A	N/A	−36.6	−27.6	−36.5	......	......	......	......	......	......	......	......	......
Adjustments pursuant to section 101(a) of BBA:														
Defense Category	N/A	N/A	+22.4	+22.4	......	......	......	......	......	......	......	......	......	......
Non-Defense Category	N/A	N/A	+22.4	+22.4	......	......	......	......	......	......	......	......	......	......
Enacted adjustments pursuant to section 251(b)(2) of BBEDCA:														
OCO/GWOT:														
Security Category	+126.5	+98.7	N/A	N/A	N/A	N/A	N/A	N/A	N/A	N/A	N/A	N/A	N/A	N/A
Defense Category	N/A	N/A	+85.4	+64.5	......	......	......	......	......	......	......	......	......	......
Non-Defense Category	N/A	N/A	+6.5	+9.3	......	......	......	......	......	......	......	......	......	......
Emergency Requirements:														
Security Category	......	+7.0	N/A	N/A	N/A	N/A	N/A	N/A	N/A	N/A	N/A	N/A	N/A	N/A
Nonsecurity Category	......	+34.6	N/A	N/A	N/A	N/A	N/A	N/A	N/A	N/A	N/A	N/A	N/A	N/A
Defense Category	N/A	N/A	+0.2	+0.1	......	......	......	......	......	......	......	......	......	......
Non-Defense Category	N/A	N/A	......	+5.3	......	......	......	......	......	......	......	......	......	......
Program Integrity:														
Nonsecurity Category	+0.5	+0.5	N/A	N/A	N/A	N/A	N/A	N/A	N/A	N/A	N/A	N/A	N/A	N/A
Non-Defense Category	N/A	N/A	+0.9	+1.5	......	......	......	......	......	......	......	......	......	......

OMB SEQUESTRATION PREVIEW REPORT FOR FY 2016

Table 1. OVERVIEW OF CHANGES TO DISCRETIONARY SPENDING LIMITS AND THE PRESIDENT'S PROPOSED LIMITS IN THE 2016 BUDGET—Continued

(Discretionary budget authority in billions of dollars)

	2012	2013	2014	2015	2016	2017	2018	2019	2020	2021	2022	2023	2024	2025
Disaster Relief:														
Security Category	+6.4	+11.8	N/A	N/A	N/A	N/A	N/A	N/A	N/A	N/A	N/A	N/A	N/A	N/A
Nonsecurity Category	+4.1	....	N/A	N/A	N/A	N/A	N/A	N/A	N/A	N/A	N/A	N/A	N/A	N/A
Non-Defense Category	N/A	N/A	+5.6	+5.7	N/A	N/A	N/A	N/A	N/A	N/A	N/A	N/A	N/A	N/A
Adjustments pursuant to section 7 of Public Laws 113–76 and 113–235:														
Defense Category	N/A	N/A	+0.2	+0.0	N/A	N/A	N/A	N/A	N/A	N/A	N/A	N/A	N/A	N/A
Non-Defense Category	N/A	N/A	N/A	....	N/A	N/A	N/A	N/A	N/A	N/A	N/A	N/A	N/A	N/A
Revised Limits Included in the OMB Preview Report:														
Security Category	816.9	801.5	N/A	N/A	N/A	N/A	N/A	N/A	N/A	N/A	N/A	N/A	N/A	N/A
Nonsecurity Category	363.5	394.1	N/A	N/A	N/A	N/A	N/A	N/A	N/A	N/A	N/A	N/A	N/A	N/A
Discretionary Category	N/A	N/A	N/A	N/A	N/A	N/A	N/A	N/A	N/A	N/A	N/A	N/A	N/A	N/A
Defense Category	N/A	N/A	606.3	585.9	523.1	590.0	603.0	616.0	630.0	644.0	N/A	N/A	N/A	N/A
Non-Defense Category	N/A	N/A	504.8	514.1	493.5	541.0	553.0	566.0	578.0	590.0	N/A	N/A	N/A	N/A
President's Proposed Changes to Discretionary Limits in the 2016 Budget:														
New Budget Proposals:														
Revise and extend limits to 2025:														
Defense Category	N/A	N/A	....	....	+37.9	–17.0	–19.0	–24.0	–32.0	–34.0	+622.0	+635.0	+648.0	+661.0
Non-Defense Category	N/A	N/A	....	....	+36.5	....	–2.0	–6.0	–13.0	–14.0	+588.0	+601.0	+614.0	+627.0
Reclassification of Surface Transportation accounts:														
Non-Defense Category	N/A	N/A	....	....	–4.2	–4.3	–4.4	–4.5	–4.6	–4.7	–4.8	–4.9	–5.0	–5.1
Reduction of base SSA program integrity funding:														
Non-Defense Category	N/A	N/A	....	....	....	–0.3	–0.3	–0.3	–0.3	–0.3	–0.3	–0.3	–0.3	–0.3
Reclassification of Contract Support Costs:														
Non-Defense Category	N/A	N/A	....	....	....	–1.0	–1.0	–1.1	–1.1	–1.1	–1.1	–1.1	–1.2	–1.2
New program integrity adjustments for IRS and UI:														
Non-Defense Category	N/A	N/A	....	....	+0.7	+1.1	+1.4	+1.8	+2.2	+2.3	+2.3	+2.4	+2.4	+2.5
New wildfire suppression adjustments for Agriculture and Interior:														
Non-Defense Category	N/A	N/A	....	....	+1.1	+1.1	+1.1	+1.1	+1.1	+1.1	+1.2	+1.2	+1.2	+1.2
Anticipated adjustments pursuant to section 251(b)(2) of BBEDCA:														
OCO/GWOT:														
Defense Category	N/A	N/A	....	....	+50.9	....	....	....	....	....	....	....	....	....

Table 1. OVERVIEW OF CHANGES TO DISCRETIONARY SPENDING LIMITS AND THE PRESIDENT'S PROPOSED LIMITS IN THE 2016 BUDGET—Continued

(Discretionary budget authority in billions of dollars)

	2012	2013	2014	2015	2016	2017	2018	2019	2020	2021	2022	2023	2024	2025
Non-Defense Category	N/A	N/A	....	....	+7.0	+26.7	+26.7	+26.7	+26.7	+26.7	....	....	....	....
Program Integrity:														
Non-Defense Category	N/A	N/A	....	....	+1.6	+0.4	+0.4	+0.5	+0.5	+0.5	+0.5	+0.5	+0.6	+0.6
Disaster Relief:														
Non-Defense Category	N/A	N/A	....	....	+6.9	....	....	....	....	....	....	....	....	....
President's proposed limits in the 2016 Budget:														
Security Category	816.9	801.5	N/A	N/A	N/A	N/A	N/A	N/A	N/A	N/A	N/A	N/A	N/A	N/A
Nonsecurity Category	363.5	394.1	N/A	N/A	N/A	N/A	N/A	N/A	N/A	N/A	N/A	N/A	N/A	N/A
Discretionary Category	N/A	N/A	N/A	N/A	N/A	N/A	N/A	N/A	N/A	N/A	N/A	N/A	N/A	N/A
Defense Category	N/A	N/A	606.3	585.9	611.9	573.0	584.0	592.0	598.0	610.0	622.0	635.0	648.0	661.0
Non-Defense Category	N/A	N/A	504.8	514.1	543.0	564.6	574.9	584.2	589.5	600.5	585.8	598.8	611.8	624.8

N/A = Not Applicable

Table 2. PREVIEW REPORT DISCRETIONARY SPENDING LIMITS UNDER CURRENT LAW

(Discretionary budget authority in millions of dollars)

	2015	2016	2017	2018	2019	2020	2021
DEFENSE (OR "REVISED SECURITY") CATEGORY							
Final Sequestration Report Spending Limit	585,870	577,000	590,000	603,000	616,000	630,000	644,000
Joint Committee Enforcement Reductions pursuant to section 251A of BBEDCA:							
Defense Cap Reduction for 2016	....	–53,909	....	....	....	....	....
Preview Report Spending Limit	585,870	523,091	590,000	603,000	616,000	630,000	644,000
NON-DEFENSE (OR "REVISED NONSECURITY") CATEGORY							
Final Sequestration Report Spending Limit	514,107	530,000	541,000	553,000	566,000	578,000	590,000
Joint Committee Enforcement Reductions pursuant to section 251A of BBEDCA:							
Non-Defense Cap Reduction for 2016	....	–36,509	....	....	....	....	....
Preview Report Spending Limit	514,107	493,491	541,000	553,000	566,000	578,000	590,000
TOTAL DISCRETIONARY SPENDING							
2015 Budget Preview Report, Total Discretionary Spending	1,013,628	1,107,000	1,131,000	1,156,000	1,182,000	1,208,000	1,234,000
2015 Final Sequestration Report, Total Discretionary Spending	1,099,977	1,107,000	1,131,000	1,156,000	1,182,000	1,208,000	1,234,000
2016 Preview Report, Total Discretionary Spending	1,099,977	1,016,582	1,131,000	1,156,000	1,182,000	1,208,000	1,234,000

N/A = Not Applicable

BCA, the ATRA, and the BBA. Table 1 also summarizes the changes to these limits proposed in the 2016 Budget, which are discussed in more detail in the proposed changes and anticipated adjustments sections below.

Current Law Adjustments to Discretionary Limits

BBEDCA permits certain adjustments to the discretionary limits. Section 251(b)(1) allows for adjustments due to changes in concepts and definitions in this report, after consultation with the Congressional Budget Office and the congressional Budget Committees. Section 251(b)(2) also authorizes certain adjustments after the enactment of appropriations. At this time, OMB includes no change to the caps for concepts and definitions or adjustments pursuant to section 251(b)(2). Pursuant to section 251A of BBEDCA, reductions are required to the 2016 discretionary spending limits. The *OMB Report to the Congress on the Joint Committee Reductions for Fiscal Year 2016* provides a complete account of the calculations that determine the amount of cap reductions required to meet the Joint Committee deficit reduction requirement for 2016. Based on the estimates in that report, the defense cap is required to be reduced by $53,909 million and the non-defense cap is required to be reduced by $36,509 million. These adjustments are made to the respective current law caps in Table 2. OMB will be required to implement reductions to the discretionary caps when it issues preview reports for future years unless legislation is enacted to cancel the Joint Committee reductions. However, as discussed above, since those reductions are not required at this time and will need to be recalculated based on the estimates of direct spending programs in future Budgets, the discretionary defense and non-defense limits for 2017 through 2021 remain unadjusted at this point.

Proposed Changes to the Discretionary Limits

The BBA took an important first step towards replacing the damaging Joint Committee reductions with sensible long-term reforms, including a number of reforms proposed in previous President's Budgets.

However, the cap reductions that are now required by law to resume in 2016 do not provide sufficient resources for national security, domestic investments, and core Government functions that are required to ensure the Nation is achieving its full potential in a growing economy. With the return of Joint Committee reductions, base discretionary funding in 2016 would be at its lowest level in a decade when adjusted for inflation. The President's 2016 Budget builds on the progress made with the enactment of the BBA and the framework included in the 2015 Budget by including several proposals to revise the discretionary caps, which are all reflected in Table 3.

The Budget proposes to restore discretionary spending to levels that would continue to support economic growth, opportunity, and safety and security. These investments will be offset by a balanced package of spending cuts, tax loophole closers, and program integrity measures included in the Budget. In addition to cancelling the 2016 mandatory sequestration order and replacing the automatic mandatory reductions required in future years, the 2016 Budget adjusts upward the 2016 through 2021 defense and non-defense caps from where they otherwise would be under Joint Committee reductions. The outyear cap increases—which are shown as reductions to the preview report spending limits since, as described above, those limits have yet to be reduced pursuant to section 251A of BBEDCA—will provide modest growth for discretionary investments. Even with these investments, discretionary spending will still reach its lowest level on record as a share of GDP. The Budget provides comparable increases to the defense and non-defense caps, and extends both caps to 2025. These additional discretionary resources in 2016 and beyond will help spur economic progress, promote opportunity, and strengthen national security.

The President's Budget also includes proposed changes in concepts and definitions that would reclassify as mandatory, as part of its reauthorization proposal, certain surface transportation accounts that are currently funded from the General Fund. In addition, the Budget proposes to reclassify as mandatory Contract Support Costs in the Bureau of Indian Affairs and the Indian Health Service starting in 2017. These proposed changes are included on Table 3 and are discussed more fully in the "Budgetary Treatment of Surface Transportation Infrastructure Funding" and "Contract Support Costs" sections of the Budget Process chapter in the *Analytical Perspectives* volume of the President's 2016 Budget.

Section 251(b)(2) of BBEDCA allows for adjustment of the discretionary caps, provided that certain conditions are met and/or specific designations are provided. Several proposals included in the Budget, if enacted, would trigger these adjustments to the discretionary caps. The Budget also proposes to shift funding for one of these purposes from discretionary to mandatory and to repeal the authority to make the associated cap adjustment. These *anticipated* adjustments, shown in Table 3, include the following:

Anticipated Current Law Adjustments Pursuant to BBEDCA

Emergency Requirement and Overseas Contingency Operations/Global War on Terrorism (OCO/GWOT) Appropriations.—These adjustments are authorized by section 251(b)(2)(A) of BBEDCA and include funding for amounts that the Congress designates in law and the President subsequently so designates as being either an emergency requirement or for OCO/GWOT activities on an account-by-account basis. In 2015, $5,402 million was enacted in separate divisions of Public Law 113-235, the Consolidated and Further Continuing Appropriations Act, 2015 (CFCAA) as emergency requirements for response and preparedness efforts surrounding the outbreak of the Ebola virus in West Africa. The President's Budget does not propose any emergency funding for 2016.

Appropriations for 2015 for the Defense, Military Construction and Veterans Affairs, and State and Foreign Operations subcommittees, all included in the CFCAA, provided a total of $73,482 million (including rescissions) for OCO/GWOT purposes for 2015, and this adjustment was made in OMB's Final Sequestration Report for 2015. In addition, Public Law 113-164, Continuing Appropriations Resolution, 2015, (the "short-term CR") which was extended through February 27, 2015 in the CFCAA, provided continuing OCO/GWOT funds for the Department of Homeland Security. For 2016, the President's Budget currently includes $57,996 million for OCO/GWOT activities for 2016, of which $7,047 million is for in-

Table 3. PROPOSED CHANGES TO THE DISCRETIONARY SPENDING LIMITS

(Discretionary budget authority in millions of dollars)

	2015	2016	2017	2018	2019	2020	2021	2022	2023	2024	2025
DEFENSE (OR "REVISED SECURITY") CATEGORY											
Preview Report Spending Limit	585,870	523,091	590,000	603,000	616,000	630,000	644,000	N/A	N/A	N/A	N/A
Revise 2016-2021 caps and extend to 2025	...	+37,909	-17,000	-19,000	-24,000	-32,000	-34,000	+622,000	+635,000	+648,000	+661,000
Anticipated adjustments pursuant to Section 251(b)(2)(A) of BBEDCA for OCO/GWOT	...	+50,949	...	...	...	...	...	...	...	...	...
Proposed Spending Limit	585,870	611,949	573,000	584,000	592,000	598,000	610,000	622,000	635,000	648,000	661,000
NON-DEFENSE (OR "REVISED NONSECURITY") CATEGORY											
Preview Report Spending Limit	514,107	493,491	541,000	553,000	566,000	578,000	590,000	N/A	N/A	N/A	N/A
Revise 2016-2021 caps and extend to 2025	...	+36,509	...	-2,000	-6,000	-13,000	-14,000	+588,000	+601,000	+614,000	+627,000
Proposed change in concepts and definitions for reclassification of general fund Transportation rail accounts	...	-4,233	-4,313	-4,396	-4,486	-4,579	-4,676	-4,769	-4,867	-4,966	-5,070
Proposed reduction of SSA base program integrity funding for CDRs and Redeterminations for shift to mandatory	...	...	-273	-273	-273	-273	-273	-273	-273	-273	-273
Proposed change in concepts and definitions for reclassification of contract support costs	...	-1,013	-1,032	-1,053	-1,074	-1,095	-1,117	-1,139	-1,163	-1,186
Anticipated and Proposed Non-Defense Adjustments for the Final Sequestration Report:											
Anticipated adjustments pursuant to Section 251(b)(2)(A) of BBEDCA for OCO/GWOT	...	+7,047	+26,666	+26,666	+26,666	+26,666	+26,666	...	...	...	...
Anticipated adjustments pursuant to Section 251(b)(2)(B) of BBEDCA for CDRs and Redeterminations	...	+1,166	...	...	...	...	...	...	...	...	...
Anticipated adjustments pursuant to Section 251(b)(2)(C) of BBEDCA for HCFAC	...	+395	+414	+434	+454	+475	+496	+518	+541	+564	+590
Anticipated adjustments pursuant to Section 251(b)(2)(D) of BBEDCA for Disaster Relief	...	+6,872	...	...	...	...	...	...	...	...	...
Proposed adjustments for Internal Revenue Service Program Integrity	...	+667	+1,035	+1,394	+1,768	+2,151	+2,213	+2,258	+2,310	+2,363	+2,418
Proposed adjustments for Unemployment Insurance Program Integrity	...	+30	+35	+40	+45	+50	+55	+60	+65	+70	+75
Proposed adjustments Agriculture and Interior Wildfire Suppression	...	+1,055	+1,076	+1,098	+1,108	+1,119	+1,143	+1,165	+1,188	+1,212	+1,236
Subtotal, Anticipated Non-Defense Adjustments	...	+17,232	+29,226	+29,632	+30,041	+30,461	+30,573	+4,001	+4,104	+4,209	+4,319
Proposed Spending Limit	514,107	542,999	564,627	574,931	584,229	589,535	600,529	585,842	598,825	611,807	624,790
TOTAL DISCRETIONARY SPENDING											
Final 2015 Sequestration Report, Total Discretionary Spending	1,099,977	1,107,000	1,131,000	1,156,000	1,182,000	1,208,000	1,234,000	N/A	N/A	N/A	N/A
Preview Report, Total Discretionary Spending	1,099,977	1,016,582	1,131,000	1,156,000	1,182,000	1,208,000	1,234,000	N/A	N/A	N/A	N/A
2016 Budget Proposed, Total Discretionary Spending	1,099,977	1,154,948	1,137,627	1,158,931	1,176,229	1,187,535	1,210,529	1,207,842	1,233,825	1,259,807	1,285,790

N/A = Not Applicable

ternational programs. The Budget also includes a cap adjustment of $26.7 billion for OCO/GWOT activities for each year in 2017 through 2021. The placeholder amounts continue to reflect a total OCO budget authority cap from 2013 to 2021 of $450 billion, in line with previous years' policy, but do not reflect any specific decisions or assumptions about OCO funding in any particular year. These amounts do not reflect the Administration's intent to transition all enduring costs currently funded in the OCO budget to the base budget beginning in 2017 and ending by 2020. Those amounts will be refined in subsequent Budgets as the Administration develops its OCO transition plan. The DOD OCO/GWOT amounts are allocated to the defense category in Table 3, while the international and outyear placeholder amounts are allocated to the nondefense category.

Continuing Disability Reviews (CDRs) and Redeterminations.—Section 251(b)(2)(B) of BBEDCA authorizes adjustment of the caps by the amounts appropriated for CDRs and redeterminations in the Social Security Administration (SSA). The maximum cap adjustment in each year is specified in BBEDCA and becomes available only if a base level, before the adjustment, of $273 million is provided for these purposes in the appropriations bill. The intent of this adjustment is to ensure sufficient resources for SSA to reduce improper payments and achieve savings in mandatory spending totaling tens of billions of dollars over the next ten years, and additional savings in the outyears. The CFCAA provided $1,123 million as a cap adjustment—which marked the second time since the caps were reinstated for 2012 that the full amount permitted under BBEDCA was provided for CDRs and redeterminations—and this adjustment was made in OMB's Final Sequestration Report for 2015. Since the adjustment for CDRs and redeterminations was fully funded in both 2014 and 2015, the 2016 Budget provides both the base funding level of $273 million and the cap adjustment level specified in BBEDCA of $1,166 million through discretionary appropriations in 2016. The $1,166 million adjustment is displayed as an anticipated adjustment to the nondefense category in Table 3. However, the failure of the Congress to provide the full level of adjustment authorized by BBEDCA prior to 2014 and the delays in annual appropriations for these activities make it difficult for the agency to achieve the targeted results in each year envisioned when the adjustments were authorized. Therefore, in order to maximize potential savings, after the transition year of 2016 the Budget proposes to provide dedicated mandatory funding for these activities starting in 2017. If mandatory funding is provided, the Budget proposes to eliminate the discretionary cap adjustment beginning in 2017 and to reduce the discretionary caps by the base funding for these activities. The mandatory funding should eliminate SSA's backlog of CDRs by the end of 2019 and prevent a new backlog from developing during the budget window. The "Program Integrity Funding" discussion in the President's Budget Reform Proposals section of the Budget Process chapter in the *Analytical Perspectives* volume of the 2016 Budget provides a complete description of this and other program integrity efforts along with OMB's methodology in determining their effectiveness.

Health Care Fraud and Abuse Control (HCFAC).—Section 251(b)(2)(C) of BBEDCA authorizes adjustment of the caps by amounts appropriated for HCFAC activities. The maximum HCFAC cap adjustment in each year is specified in BBEDCA and becomes available only if a base level of $311 million for these purposes is provided in the appropriations bill before the adjustment. In 2015, for the first time since the caps were reinstated in 2012, both the base $311 million level and the maximum cap adjustment permitted by BBEDCA were fully funded in the CFCAA, and OMB's Final Sequestration Report for 2015 included an adjustment of $361 million (the 2015 cap adjustment specified in BBEDCA) for this funding. The 2016 Budget fully funds the base amount for this program and includes the full cap adjustment of $395 million permitted by BBEDCA for 2016 and cap adjustments aligned with BBEDCA for each year thereafter. The "Program Integrity Funding" discussion in the President's Budget Reform Proposals section of the Budget Process chapter in the *Analytical Perspectives* volume of the 2016 Budget provides a complete description of this and other program integrity efforts and OMB's methodology in determining their effectiveness.

Disaster Funding.—Section 251(b)(2)(D) of BBEDCA authorizes an adjustment to the caps for appropriations that are designated by the Congress as being for "disaster relief," which is defined as activities carried out pursuant to a determination under section 102(2) of the Robert T. Stafford Disaster Relief and Emergency Assistance Act (42 U.S.C. 5122(2)). BBEDCA sets a limit for the adjustment equal to the total of the average funding provided for disaster relief over the previous 10 years (excluding the highest and lowest years), plus any portion of the allowable adjustment (funding ceiling) for the previous year that was not appropriated (excluding the portion of the previous year's ceiling that was itself due to any unused amount from the year before). For the 2015 adjustment, OMB determined a preview estimate of $18,430 million, and the Congress provided continuing appropriations of $5,626 million for the Federal Emergency Management Agency's (FEMA's) Disaster Relief Fund (DRF) account in the short-term CR and a total of $91 million for the Department of Agriculture's Emergency Forest Restoration Program, Emergency Conservation Program, and Watershed and Flood Prevention Operations accounts in the CFCAA. OMB's Final Sequestration Report for 2015 allocated these combined adjustments of $5,717 million to the non-defense category. The amounts provided as full-year or continuing appropriations for 2015 are $12,713 million below the allowable adjustment. However, pursuant to section 251(b)(2)(D)(i)(II) of BBEDCA, any unused carryover from 2014 ($6,517 million) cannot carry forward into the calculation of the 2016 preview estimate. As a result, only $6,196 million of this total underage will carry forward into the calculation of the 2016 preview adjustment in OMB's August 2015 Sequestration Update Report for Fiscal Year 2016 if no further appropriations are provided for disaster relief in 2015 that are designated for disaster relief, and if the current continuing appropriation remains unchanged when final appropriations for the Department of Homeland Security are completed. The 2016 Budget requests $6,872 million in funding in two accounts to be designated for disaster relief by the Congress: $6,713 million in FEMA's DRF to cover the costs of Presidentially-declared major disasters, including identified costs for previously declared catastrophic events and the predictable annual cost of non-catastrophic events expected to obligate in 2016, and $159 million in the Small Business Administration's Disaster Loans Program Account for administrative expenses. Both of these amounts are shown on Table 3 as an anticipated cap adjustment to the non-defense category. See "Disaster Relief Funding" in the President's Budget Reform Proposals section of the Budget Process chapter in the *Analytical Perspectives* volume of the 2016 Budget for a full description of this adjustment and the Administration's 2016 Request.

New Cap Adjustment Proposals

Program Integrity.—In addition to the adjustments discussed above, the 2016 Budget proposes to amend section 251(b)(2) of BBEDCA by adding two new discretionary cap adjustments related to program integrity efforts. These new adjustments are for tax enforcement, including tax compliance to address the Federal tax gap, via the Internal Revenue Service's (IRS) Enforcement and Operations Support accounts and the Alcohol and Tobacco Tax and Trade Bureau (TTB), and for in-person reemployment and eligibility assessments, unemployment insurance improper payment reviews, and reemployment services by the Department of Labor. The adjustments would be permitted if the underlying appropriations bill provides a base level of funding for these activities. These new adjustments total $667 million for IRS and TTB and $30 million for Labor in 2016 and are included in Table 3 as proposed adjustments to the non-defense limits in all years. For more information on these new adjustments, see the "Program Integrity Funding" section of the Budget Process chapter of the Analytical Perspectives volume of the 2016 Budget.

Wildfire Suppression Operations.—The 2016 Budget also proposes to amend section 251(b)(2) of BBEDCA by adding a new discretionary cap adjustment for wildfire suppression operations at the Departments of Agriculture and the Interior. The proposal allows for a maximum permissible adjustment of $1.5 billion in 2016 that increases to $2.7 billion by 2022 and remains at that level thereafter. The adjustment is permitted if the underlying appropriations bill provides a base funding level equal to 70 percent of the average costs for wildfire suppression operations over the previous 10 years to ensure that the cap adjustment is only used for the most severe fire activity, since it is one percent of fires that cause 30 percent of costs. The permissible adjustment is a ceiling, not a target. Moreover, the adjustment would not increase overall discretionary spending because the existing disaster relief cap adjustment ceiling would be reduced by the amount provided for wildfire suppression operations under the cap adjustment for the preceding fiscal year. At this time, the Administration is requesting that only $1.1 billion be funded by the wildfire suppression operations cap adjustment in 2016 ($855 million in Agriculture and $200 million in Interior), which is shown as a proposed adjustment to the non-defense limits in all years. If the cap adjustment is enacted, additional requests might be transmitted at a later time, as additional information about the severity of the fire season becomes known. For 2017 through 2025, the cap adjustment levels are placeholders that increase at the policy growth rates in the President's Budget. Those amounts will be refined in subsequent Budgets as data on the average costs for wildfire suppression are updated annually. For more information on this new adjustment, see the "Proposed Adjustment to the Discretionary Spending Limits for Wildfire Suppression Operations at the Departments of Agriculture and the Interior" section of the Budget Process chapter of the Analytical Perspectives volume of the 2016 Budget.

Table 1. OVERVIEW OF CHANGES TO DISCRETIONARY SPENDING LIMITS AND THE PRESIDENT'S PROPOSED LIMITS IN THE 2016 BUDGET

(Discretionary budget authority in billions of dollars)

	2012	2013	2014	2015	2016	2017	2018	2019	2020	2021	2022	2023	2024	2025
Original limits set in Title I of the Budget Control Act of 2011:														
Security Category	684.0	686.0	N/A	N/A	N/A	N/A	N/A	N/A	N/A	N/A	N/A	N/A	N/A	N/A
Nonsecurity Category	359.0	361.0	N/A	N/A	N/A	N/A	N/A	N/A	N/A	N/A	N/A	N/A	N/A	N/A
Discretionary Category	N/A	N/A	1,066.0	1,086.0	1,107.0	1,131.0	1,156.0	1,182.0	1,208.0	1,234.0	N/A	N/A	N/A	N/A
Redefinition of limits pursuant to section 251A of BBEDCA:														
Security Category		-686.0	N/A	N/A	N/A	N/A	N/A	N/A	N/A	N/A	N/A	N/A	N/A	N/A
Nonsecurity Category		-361.0	N/A	N/A	N/A	N/A	N/A	N/A	N/A	N/A	N/A	N/A	N/A	N/A
Discretionary Category	N/A	N/A	-1,066.0	-1,086.0	-1,107.0	-1,131.0	-1,156.0	-1,182.0	-1,208.0	-1,234.0	N/A	N/A	N/A	N/A
Defense Category	N/A	N/A	+556.0	+566.0	+577.0	+590.0	+603.0	+616.0	+630.0	+644.0	N/A	N/A	N/A	N/A
Non-Defense Category	N/A	N/A	+510.0	+520.0	+530.0	+541.0	+553.0	+566.0	+578.0	+590.0	N/A	N/A	N/A	N/A
Adjustments to limits pursuant to section 901(d) of ATRA:														
Security Category		+684.0	N/A	N/A	N/A	N/A	N/A	N/A	N/A	N/A	N/A	N/A	N/A	N/A
Nonsecurity Category		+359.0	N/A	N/A	N/A	N/A	N/A	N/A	N/A	N/A	N/A	N/A	N/A	N/A
Defense Category	N/A	N/A	-4.0											
Non-Defense Category	N/A	N/A	-4.0											
Joint Select Committee on Deficit Reduction Enforcement:														
Defense Category	N/A	N/A	-53.9	-44.7	-53.9									
Non-Defense Category	N/A	N/A	-36.6	-27.6	-36.5									
Adjustments pursuant to section 101(a) of BBA:														
Defense Category	N/A	N/A	+22.4											
Non-Defense Category	N/A	N/A	+22.4											
Enacted adjustments pursuant to section 251(b)(2) of BBEDCA:														
OCO/GWOT:														
Security Category	+126.5	+98.7	N/A	N/A	N/A	N/A	N/A	N/A	N/A	N/A	N/A	N/A	N/A	N/A
Defense Category	N/A	N/A	+85.4	+64.5	N/A	N/A	N/A	N/A	N/A	N/A	N/A	N/A	N/A	N/A
Non-Defense Category	N/A	N/A	+6.5	+9.3	N/A	N/A	N/A	N/A	N/A	N/A	N/A	N/A	N/A	N/A
Emergency Requirements:														
Security Category		+7.0	N/A	N/A	N/A	N/A	N/A	N/A	N/A	N/A	N/A	N/A	N/A	N/A
Nonsecurity Category		+34.6	N/A	N/A	N/A	N/A	N/A	N/A	N/A	N/A	N/A	N/A	N/A	N/A
Defense Category	N/A	N/A	+0.2	+0.1	N/A	N/A	N/A	N/A	N/A	N/A	N/A	N/A	N/A	N/A
Non-Defense Category	N/A	N/A		+5.3	N/A	N/A	N/A	N/A	N/A	N/A	N/A	N/A	N/A	N/A
Program Integrity:														
Nonsecurity Category	+0.5	+0.5	N/A	N/A	N/A	N/A	N/A	N/A	N/A	N/A	N/A	N/A	N/A	N/A
Non-Defense Category	N/A	N/A	+0.9	+1.5	N/A	N/A	N/A	N/A	N/A	N/A	N/A	N/A	N/A	N/A
Disaster Relief:														
Security Category	+6.4	+11.8	N/A	N/A	N/A	N/A	N/A	N/A	N/A	N/A	N/A	N/A	N/A	N/A
Nonsecurity Category	+4.1		N/A	N/A	N/A	N/A	N/A	N/A	N/A	N/A	N/A	N/A	N/A	N/A
Non-Defense Category	N/A	N/A	+5.6	+5.7	N/A	N/A	N/A	N/A	N/A	N/A	N/A	N/A	N/A	N/A
Adjustments pursuant to section 7 of Public Laws 113-76 and 113-235:														
Defense Category	N/A	N/A	+0.2	+0.0							N/A	N/A	N/A	N/A
Non-Defense Category	N/A	N/A									N/A	N/A	N/A	N/A

Table 1. OVERVIEW OF CHANGES TO DISCRETIONARY SPENDING LIMITS AND THE PRESIDENT'S PROPOSED LIMITS IN THE 2016 BUDGET

(Discretionary budget authority in billions of dollars)

	2012	2013	2014	2015	2016	2017	2018	2019	2020	2021	2022	2023	2024	2025
Revised Limits Included in the OMB Preview Report:														
Security Category..................	816.9	801.5	N/A	N/A	N/A	N/A	N/A	N/A	N/A	N/A	N/A	N/A	N/A	N/A
Nonsecurity Category............	363.5	394.1	N/A	N/A	N/A	N/A	N/A	N/A	N/A	N/A	N/A	N/A	N/A	N/A
Discretionary Category.........	N/A	N/A	N/A	N/A	N/A	N/A	N/A	N/A	N/A	N/A	N/A	N/A	N/A	N/A
Defense Category...................	N/A	N/A	606.3	585.9	523.1	590.0	603.0	616.0	630.0	644.0	N/A	N/A	N/A	N/A
Non-Defense Category...........	N/A	N/A	504.8	514.1	493.5	541.0	553.0	566.0	578.0	590.0	N/A	N/A	N/A	N/A
President's Proposed Changes to Discretionary Limits in the 2016 Budget:														
New Budget Proposals:														
Revise and extend limits to 2025:														
Defense Category...................	N/A	N/A	....	....	+37.9	-17.0	-19.0	-24.0	-32.0	-34.0	+622.0	+635.0	+648.0	+661.0
Non-Defense Category...........	N/A	N/A	....	....	+36.5	....	-2.0	-6.0	-13.0	-14.0	+588.0	+601.0	+614.0	+627.0
Reclassification of Surface Transportation accounts:														
Non-Defense Category...........	N/A	N/A	....	....	-4.2	-4.3	-4.4	-4.5	-4.6	-4.7	-4.8	-4.9	-5.0	-5.1
Reduction of base SSA program integrity funding:														
Non-Defense Category...........	N/A	N/A	....	....	....	-0.3	-0.3	-0.3	-0.3	-0.3	-0.3	-0.3	-0.3	-0.3
Reclassification of Contract Support Costs:														
Non-Defense Category...........	N/A	N/A	....	....	....	-1.0	-1.0	-1.1	-1.1	-1.1	-1.1	-1.1	-1.2	-1.2
New program integrity adjustments for IRS and UI:														
Non-Defense Category...........	N/A	N/A	....	....	+0.7	+1.1	+1.4	+1.8	+2.2	+2.3	+2.3	+2.4	+2.4	+2.5
New wildfire suppression adjustments for Agriculture and Interior:														
Non-Defense Category...........	N/A	N/A	....	....	+1.1	+1.1	+1.1	+1.1	+1.1	+1.1	+1.2	+1.2	+1.2	+1.2
Anticipated adjustments pursuant to section 251(b)(2) of BBEDCA:														
OCO/GWOT:														
Defense Category...................	N/A	N/A	....	....	+50.9	....	....	....	....	....	....	....	....	....
Non-Defense Category...........	N/A	N/A	....	....	+7.0	+26.7	+26.7	+26.7	+26.7	+26.7	....	....	....	....
Program Integrity:														
Non-Defense Category...........	N/A	N/A	....	....	+1.6	+0.4	+0.4	+0.5	+0.5	+0.5	+0.5	+0.5	+0.6	+0.6
Disaster Relief:														
Non-Defense Category...........	N/A	N/A	....	....	+6.9	....	....	....	....	....	....	....	....	....
President's proposed limits in the 2016 Budget:														
Security Category..................	816.9	801.5	N/A	N/A	N/A	N/A	N/A	N/A	N/A	N/A	N/A	N/A	N/A	N/A
Nonsecurity Category............	363.5	394.1	N/A	N/A	N/A	N/A	N/A	N/A	N/A	N/A	N/A	N/A	N/A	N/A
Discretionary Category.........	N/A	N/A	N/A	N/A	N/A	N/A	N/A	N/A	N/A	N/A	N/A	N/A	N/A	N/A
Defense Category...................	N/A	N/A	606.3	585.9	611.9	573.0	584.0	592.0	598.0	610.0	622.0	635.0	648.0	661.0
Non-Defense Category...........	N/A	N/A	504.8	514.1	543.0	564.6	574.9	584.2	589.5	600.5	585.8	598.8	611.8	624.8

N/A = Not Applicable

Table 2. PREVIEW REPORT DISCRETIONARY SPENDING LIMITS UNDER CURRENT LAW
(Discretionary budget authority in millions of dollars)

	2015	2016	2017	2018	2019	2020	2021
DEFENSE (OR "REVISED SECURITY") CATEGORY							
Final Sequestration Report Spending Limit.............	585,870	577,000	590,000	603,000	616,000	630,000	644,000
Joint Committee Enforcement Reductions pursuant to section 251A of BBEDCA: Defense Cap Reduction for 2016........	………	-53,909	………	………	………	………	………
Preview Report Spending Limit...............................	585,870	523,091	590,000	603,000	616,000	630,000	644,000
NON-DEFENSE (OR "REVISED NONSECURITY") CATEGORY							
Final Sequestration Report Spending Limit.............	514,107	530,000	541,000	553,000	566,000	578,000	590,000
Joint Committee Enforcement Reductions pursuant to section 251A of BBEDCA: Non-Defense Cap Reduction for 2016....	………	-36,509	………	………	………	………	………
Preview Report Spending Limit...............................	514,107	493,491	541,000	553,000	566,000	578,000	590,000
TOTAL DISCRETIONARY SPENDING							
2015 Budget Preview Report, Total Discretionary Spending................................	1,013,628	1,107,000	1,131,000	1,156,000	1,182,000	1,208,000	1,234,000
2015 Final Sequestration Report, Total Discretionary Spending................................	1,099,977	1,107,000	1,131,000	1,156,000	1,182,000	1,208,000	1,234,000
2016 Preview Report, Total Discretionary Spending................................	1,099,977	1,016,582	1,131,000	1,156,000	1,182,000	1,208,000	1,234,000

N/A = Not Applicable

Table 3. PROPOSED CHANGES TO THE DISCRETIONARY SPENDING LIMITS

(Discretionary budget authority in millions of dollars)

	2015	2016	2017	2018	2019	2020	2021	2022	2023	2024	2025
DEFENSE (OR "REVISED SECURITY") CATEGORY											
Preview Report Spending Limit	585,870	523,091	590,000	603,000	616,000	630,000	644,000	N/A	N/A	N/A	N/A
Revise 2016-2021 caps and extend to 2025		-37,909	-17,000	-19,000	-24,000	-32,000	-34,000	+622,000	+635,000	+648,000	+661,000
Anticipated adjustments pursuant to Section 251(b)(2)(A) of BBEDCA for OCO/GWOT		-50,949									
Proposed Spending Limit	585,870	611,949	573,000	584,000	592,000	598,000	610,000	622,000	635,000	648,000	661,000
NON-DEFENSE (OR "REVISED NONSECURITY") CATEGORY											
Preview Report Spending Limit	514,107	493,491	541,000	553,000	566,000	578,000	590,000	N/A	N/A	N/A	N/A
Revise 2016-2021 caps and extend to 2025		-36,509		-2,000	-6,000	-13,000	-14,000	+588,000	+601,000	+614,000	+627,000
Proposed change in concepts and definitions for reclassification of general fund Transportation rail accounts		-4,233	-4,313	-4,396	-4,486	-4,579	-4,676	-4,769	-4,867	-4,966	-5,070
Proposed reduction of SSA base program integrity funding for CDRs and Redeterminations for shift to mandatory			-273	-273	-273	-273	-273	-273	-273	-273	-273
Proposed change in concepts and definitions for reclassification of contract support costs			-1,013	-1,032	-1,053	-1,074	-1,095	-1,117	-1,139	-1,163	-1,186
Anticipated and Proposed Non-Defense Adjustments for the Final Sequestration Report:											
Anticipated adjustments pursuant to Section 251(b)(2)(A) of BBEDCA for OCO/GWOT		+7,047	+26,666	+26,666	+26,666	+26,666	+26,666				
Anticipated adjustments pursuant to Section 251(b)(2)(B) of BBEDCA for CDRs and Redeterminations		+1,166									
Anticipated adjustments pursuant to Section 251(b)(2)(C) of BBEDCA for HCFAC		+395	+414	+434	+454	+475	+496	+518	+541	+564	+590
Anticipated adjustments pursuant to Section 251(b)(2)(D) of BBEDCA for Disaster Relief		+6,872									
Proposed adjustments for Internal Revenue Service Program Integrity		+667	+1,035	+1,394	+1,768	+2,151	+2,213	+2,258	+2,310	+2,363	+2,418
Proposed adjustments for Unemployment Insurance Program Integrity		+30	+35	+40	+45	+50	+55	+60	+65	+70	+75
Proposed adjustments Agriculture and Interior Wildfire Suppression		+1,055	+1,076	+1,098	+1,108	+1,119	+1,143	+1,165	+1,188	+1,212	+1,236
Subtotal, Anticipated Non-Defense Adjustments		+17,232	+29,226	+29,632	+30,041	+30,461	+30,573	+4,001	+4,104	+4,209	+4,319
Proposed Spending Limit	514,107	542,999	564,627	574,931	584,229	589,535	600,529	585,842	598,825	611,807	624,790

Table 3. PROPOSED CHANGES TO THE DISCRETIONARY SPENDING LIMITS
(Discretionary budget authority in millions of dollars)

	2015	2016	2017	2018	2019	2020	2021	2022	2023	2024	2025
TOTAL DISCRETIONARY SPENDING											
Final 2015 Sequestration Report,											
Total Discretionary Spending	1,099,977	1,107,000	1,131,000	1,156,000	1,182,000	1,208,000	1,234,000	N/A	N/A	N/A	N/A
Preview Report,											
Total Discretionary Spending	1,099,977	1,016,582	1,131,000	1,156,000	1,182,000	1,208,000	1,234,000	N/A	N/A	N/A	N/A
2016 Budget Proposed,											
Total Discretionary Spending	1,099,977	1,154,948	1,137,627	1,158,931	1,176,229	1,187,535	1,210,529	1,207,842	1,233,825	1,259,807	1,285,790

N/A = Not Applicable

www.ingramcontent.com/pod-product-compliance
Lightning Source LLC
Chambersburg PA
CBHW080535190526
45169CB00008B/3183